# 60 Minute

# Scrum

STEWART LANCASTER

ISBN- 1496142489

ISBN-978-1496142481

# CONTENTS

# PREFACE

Too fast, too soon...

Anyone working in the projects space today will no doubt be familiar with the pressure to deliver too much with too few resources. This book has been written with this in mind. This is not a substitute for ongoing and indeed lifelong learning in the scrum arena, but instead is designed to provide an introduction to the Scrum framework and provide you with a breakdown of the core scrum principles.

More specifically this book is designed to help you not only learn the principles of scrum in less than 60 minutes, but to impress as much of this framework into your long term memory as possible so you can begin applying these principles.

A bit of a challenging task perhaps, to learn a new way of working, a new way of thinking in less time than it takes to watch a movie, but one that I am sure, if you are reading this that you have the appetite, the determination and the will to complete this task.

In writing this book, I have had to use a number of cutting edge models based in the field of neuro-science to try and deeply implant everything you read in the next 60 minutes into your long term memory including connecting left brain (reading, writing, listening, logic and sequence) and right brain (images, colour, music, creativity and intuition), a phenomenon known as the "primary" and "recency" effect and finally a number of memory consolidation techniques.

The brain has a four step process which is always followed in the formation of every new memory:

Encoding > Consolidation > Storage > Retrieval

| Encoding: | This is the process of reading or learning the new material |
|---|---|
| Consolidation: | This is where the newly learnt information is repeated, often in different forms to the point where you feel you have 'memorised' the information (short term memory only) |
| Storage: | This is where the information is moved into your long term memory |
| Retrieval: | The ability to recall the information at will |

The techniques described above focus predominantly in the memory consolidation stage, which increases the likelihood of forming long term memories.

To help aid this process and ensure your success you may wish to do the following:

Avoid distraction: Don't get me wrong, you WILL lose focus and you WILL be distracted during the course of this book, this is simply human nature and more importantly the nature of our brains. You can minimise these effects by reading somewhere you will not be too distracted that is not too noisy to concentrate.

Repetition: Try to repeat the models and methods you learn in this book, say them out loud, write and re-write them until you are able to recall them without looking at the text. Repeating this exercise within the next 24 and 48 hours will help in transferring these memories into your long term memory (memory encoding, consolidation and storage)

Chunking: Your brain has the ability to focus for finite periods and tends to recall more at the beginning and the end of a sequence. Beyond this, memory recall is diminished. Use this inherent feature to your advantage and try to break this book down into smaller, more memorable chunks (as a rule of thumb to calculate your optimum focus period you should use your age plus or minus two minutes) creating multiple start/stop points. Take a five to fifteen minute break between sections and review what you have read, draw diagrams or simply go for a walk. These are all ways of supporting the memory creation process.

Highlight: Use the highlighting feature in your e-reader to draw attention to specific parts of the text, this will help you recall key points and will further aid future repetition, if you have time use these highlighted session to create cheat sheets that will allow you to anchor the method into your brain, doodle and scribble away until your heart's content but most of all, enjoy.

Listen to Music: You may think that this contradicts the previous advice to avoid distractions but the link between (certain types of) music and increased memory recall is well documented and widely accepted (often referred to as the 'Mozart Effect'). Quietly playing classical music in the background or through headphones can increase your ability to concentrate for longer periods.

Doodle: As you come across concepts in this book draw diagrams, create pictures and models to help you remember what you have learnt. Use pictures, colours, make the funny, obscure, fantastical, rude and personal to ensure that these are a powerful aid to recall.

As with all of these suggestions, try them, use whatever works, and file the rest for future use; this is all about building long terms memories to support your endeavors.

# 1 THE SCRUM PARADOX

Scrum is a light weight framework built predominantly on Agile principles which has often been described as "easy to learn, hard to master". It has gained popularity as it is incredibly simple to understand for both users and stakeholders and it addresses a number of pitfalls with standard project management and software design methodologies.

One of the key principles of Scrum is that it allows a team to deliver the highest value in the shortest space of time, often in uncertain or continually changing environments; importantly Scrum accommodates and even embraces change, allowing organisations to quickly adapt to the needs of their clients or the actions of their competitors.

Whilst the Scrum framework has gained most popularity within the software / technology sector, the framework is not tied inherently to any discipline and could equally be applied to projects in any business area. Scrum flies in the face of many of the alternatives models including the well known Waterfall model which relies on a series of sequential steps in the development process to deliver a defined end result.

This change in approach can often be difficult for organisations to accept as it feels counter intuitive however the reduced feedback loop found within Scrum allows for feedback to be received far earlier in the process compared with alternative approaches; allowing for changes and other corrections to be made far sooner in the process.

This approach is intrinsically understood by clients who expect their teams to be able to respond effectively to newly identified and changing requirements. Scrum can even go as far as to provide the organisation with a competitive advantage allowing it to embrace a new technology or approach much faster than a number of its competitors in a controlled fashion.

Scrum Vs. traditional delivery approaches:

- Individuals and interactions over processes and tools

- Working software over comprehensive documentation

- Customer collaboration over contract negotiation

- Responding to change over following a plan

(Source: Agile values – available at http://agilemanifesto.org/)

Summary:

In summary, Scrum uses sprints which are far shorter in duration than comparable approaches with defined, high value outputs at the end. It lends itself to environments where quality criteria are less well defined or where constant change requests are received. It allows organisations to deliver incremental value at an accelerated pace without the need to police staff.

The framework consists of 3 defined Roles, 3 prescribed Artefacts and 5 defined Activities and relies on the whole team working together rather than handoffs between functional roles or defined stages working towards a common goal.

# 60 MINUTE SCRUM

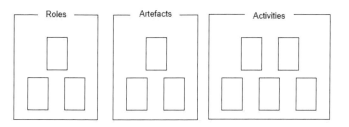

# 2 SCRUM ROLES

Scrum teams are unique in contrast to other project management methodologies in that they are self-organising, cross functional in terms of skillsets and have the autonomy to decide how they intend to achieve the team's goals. There are only three recognised roles within the Scrum framework:

| Product Owner | Scrum Master | Team Member |
|---|---|---|

Part of the challenge in adopting a Scrum approach is letting go of the established organisation hierarchy and thinking in terms of roles instead of job titles and functions. This can be a cultural step too far for some key stakeholders but is a core part of the Scrum framework.

## Product owner

The product owner is the individual responsible for achieving the best return on investment for the firm. They do this by directing the efforts of the team to ensure that the focus is always on prioritising higher value / higher impact work over lower value / lower impact work.

As such the product owner if responsible for the planning and prioritisation of the work included in each sprint; and ultimately the finished product. The product owner is the only person who has the authority to reprioritise any of the work in the product backlog.

As the individual ultimately responsible for the success of the end result it is down to the product owner to ensure that all of the client requirements are fully understood by the team members. The way this is done in Scrum is through user stories. User stories are a way of defining requirement that are intuitive for key stakeholders to disseminate in detail without having to understand the Scrum framework.

"As a [insert stakeholder], I want [insert feature], so I can [insert benefit]".

Whilst this formula is simple, it clearly identifies key stakeholders, the desired features and the benefits of deploying these features, this could be further simplified as essentially as feature and benefit can be summed up as incremental added value. Essentially when we use user stories, we build a picture of value from the stakeholder's point of view and which in turn allows the Scrum team to focus exclusively on areas deemed more important.

User stories allow us to build a clearer picture about the desired value from the various stakeholders (stakeholder map). Each story is added to the product backlog; the idea behind each user story is that it identifies the value desired by the customer or stakeholder in terms of features or outcomes, generally the user story allows freedom for the team members to agree the most effective way of achieving this desired outcome without being too prescriptive; essentially the focus is on the desired outcome rather than the process of getting there.

**Product owner summary:**

- Owns the vision of the product

- Represents (and in some cases is) the customer

- Owns and maintains the product backlog

- Is responsible for the prioritisation of work for the team members

**Scrum Master**

The Scrum master is often the most misunderstood role within the Scrum framework and can be summed up as a "servant leader". His primary role is to remove any roadblocks for the team members to help them deliver the desired output within the sprint.

The Scrum master is essentially an expert in the Scrum framework, they act as the Scrum advocate within the organisation and provide coaching and guidance to all other members of the Scrum team. They are often required to facilitate the smooth running of Scrum activities as required and are responsible for ensuring that the team remains efficient in the goals they have selected, whist the team members remains accountable for delivering their goals

As mentioned previously, Scrum teams are by definition self-organising, meaning that team members will generally be expected to manage their own time and as a consequence they will not be micro managed by the Scrum master.

The Scrum master will guide the team and ensure they work within a Scrum Framework, and will often have the responsibility of encouraging the correct behaviors from both the team members and the product owner whilst trying to promote the benefits and therefore the acceptance of Scrum within the organisation.

Scrum master Summary:

- Removes road blocks

- Is a "servant leader" and peer of the team members

- Is an expert in the Scrum methodology

**Team Member**

Sometimes referred to as the 'development team', the role of the Scrum team member is not as self explanatory as it first seems, often with cross-functional individuals working closely (or interchangeably) on the same piece of work, rather than having defined, individuals roles and goals.

It is down to the team (collectively and individually) to decide how they intend to achieve the desired end result defined in the user stories. In short they have total authority over how the work is done.

Whilst holding full responsibility and accountability for the work being done, the team members are responsible for creating the estimates for the completion of each of the user stories and ultimately the work schedules. It is important to note that responsibility for achieving the team's Goals are held collectively, not individually amongst the team members,

The challenge when composing the team

(usually the role of the Scrum master) is to ensure that all of the required skills are possessed by the team members. Remember the focus of the team is to deliver a "potentially shippable product increment" at the end of each sprint so the team must possess all of the skills required to deliver a functional product at the end of the sprint; in practice this often means recruiting a combination of 'specialist' and 'generalist' individuals.

The optimum team size is often considered to be seven, plus or minus two individuals. Anything less than three individuals would general result in too little activity within the sprint to be considered useful and anything over nine is considered unruly.

Team Member Summary:

- Team members are self-organising

- Responsible for delivering the value defined within the user stories

- It is generally accepted that Scrum teams should be no more than 5 to 9 individuals; any team - larger than this should be split into two smaller, self organising teams.

**Scrum Roles Summary:**

Product owner: – Responsible for determine priority of the work to be done

Scrum master: – Responsible for ensuring the team remains efficient, removing any blocks preventing the work being completed. Owns the Scrum framework and ensures all other roles are operating correctly

Team member: – Responsible for how the work is done and responsible for delivering the sprint goals

**Remember:**

To help you remember the three Scrum roles, think of the word PoST, this graphic below is designed to anchor this mnemonic into your long term memory. To aid this process, draw the signpost image and write and re-write the word PoST (maintaining capitalisation); repeat this process in one day and then again in one week to push this into your long term memory.

# P<sub>o</sub>ST

Product owner

Scrum Master

Team Member

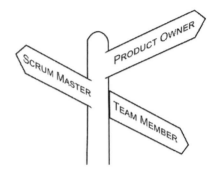

# 3 SCRUM ARTEFACTS

There are three prescribed artefacts within the Scrum framework:

## Product backlog

The product backlog is a list of all outstanding backlog items for the product / project, they are usually ordered from highest value to the lowest value in the form of User stories (the terms user story and backlog item are generally interchangeable). User stories are a simple and intuitive way of describing requirements to the Scrum team. It allows the product owner (or ultimate end customer) to explain a desired end result, leaving the team members the autonomy to deliver the desired value in the most effective way.

Remember the user story formula provided earlier:

"As a [insert stakeholder], I want [insert feature], so I can [insert benefit]".

This can be simplified to [stakeholder], [feature] + [benefit]

Examples of User stories in action are as follows:

"As a new customer of the website, I want to be able to place an item in my shopping basket that will allow me to come back and review this item later before deciding to purchase".

"As a busy investor, I want to be able to see my stock portfolio on my smartphone any time, day or night"

There are a number of variations on the format of user stories but the important thing is that the stakeholder and stakeholder value required is clearly identified.

It is common for the product backlog to be

segregated into  new features, change requests and bugs (in a software project), whilst some teams find it useful to draw these distinctions the decision to include a backlog item should always be based on the highest value items; as such many team remove such labels. The key here is to find out what works well within the culture of your organisation, examples of backlog item information include:

- Risk

- Certainty (or uncertainty)

- Value (business value or client value)

- Dependencies

- Date Needed

- Resource required (effort)

product owners may decide not to physically re-order the product backlog but would instead choose to assign a priority value such as a number between 1 and 10, this approach is effective where a spreadsheet or dedicated Scrum software is in use and allows the product owner to quickly identify a range of higher priority backlog items to include in the next sprint (Further information on Scrum software can be found in Chapter 8: Scrum Resources

There is no right or wrong way of prioritising the product backlog, but whatever method is used the team must ensure that the method reflects the product owners (and indirectly the end client if different) priorities.

Where the product owner adopts a 'white board' approach, physical reordering of the backlog items based on their value (i.e. moving high priority items to the top of the list) can not only provide a constant visual reminder in the office as to the number of activities being undertaken (and therefore the value being delivered over the course of the project) but also provides stakeholders insight into the delivery pipeline.

The product backlog can be amended by anyone inside or outside of the team; however it is the responsibility of the product owner to order the backlog items accordingly.

## Sprint backlog

The sprint backlog (sometimes referred to as the release backlog) is a smaller, more focused version of the product backlog that contains only backlog items that the team members have committed to deliver during the current (or upcoming) sprint. Often these stories are broken down into smaller tasks which will have an estimation for completion against it. The sprint backlog is the closest thing you will find to a traditional project plan within the Scrum framework, but will only provide high level commitments within the existing sprint; it makes no commitment to deliver any work in subsequent sprints until the start of the sprint.

One of the key differences between this and the product backlog is that the team members determine which items make it into the sprint backlog based on their estimation of their ability to successfully deliver the value within the upcoming sprint.

**Estimation techniques:**

When you have a number of team members working together, it is essential to deploy a common unit of resource measurement; there are two widely accepted estimation techniques in Scrum:

- Time

- Story points

Typically when using time, team members

are forced to select one of a number of pre determined values (such as 1h, 2h, 4h, 8h, 1d, 2d etc) and no time estimation outside of these established amounts will be accepted.

Story points are an arbitrary but elegant solution which allows the team to estimate the complexity of a backlog item (or task). Over a period of time, tracking the number of story points completed during a significant period will produce the team velocity. This provides a frame of reference as to how much the team is able to accomplish during an 'average' sprint.

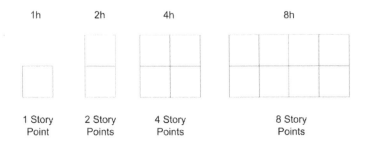

1h  2h  4h  8h

1 Story Point  2 Story Points  4 Story Points  8 Story Points

Sprint Velocity

Sprint velocity = number of story points delivered in the last sprint

Sprint Velocity is a useful way to measure the pace of delivery for the team and is essentially an average number of User stories completed over a number of previous sprints. This number can be used as a guide by the team members as an objective guide to help them ensure they select the optimum number of backlog items during the sprint Planning Meeting (see Chapter 4. Scrum Activities).

Potentially Shippable product Increment

Often referred to simply as an "Increment"; this is the third and final Scrum artefact, and is essentially the reason that the Scrum framework exists... to ultimately deliver something of value! An increment is essentially the cumulative total of all of the work completed (backlog items) during the current sprint. The key here is that the work should be of sufficient quality to be potentially shippable, in practice this means complete and (ideally) without defect.

To put this in to the context of a software project, an example of potentially shippable could be a customer website, built and tested based on the customer requirements (user stories) which is ready to go into a live environment. It may not necessarily be live and in fact there may be an internal process that the IT department has to go through in order to move the site to live.

Scrum does not required vast amounts of additional supporting information other than the delivery of the product increment itself. Where supporting documentation is required by the user, this should be defined in the product backlog and estimations on the resource required to produce the above should have been included in the sprint.

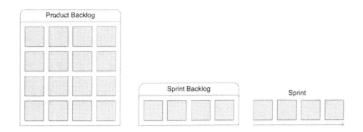

## Summary:

The product backlog is owned by the product owner

The sprint backlog is owned by the team members

The Increment is owned by the whole Scrum team

## Remember:

The acronym for the Scrum artefacts is 'PSI', this is also the name of a Greek letter

(Ψ) pronounced "sai"; it is a three pronged letter which can be useful in remembering the three Scrum artefacts. Draw the letter PSI repeatedly including the letter at the top until you have committed it to memory, repeat this process in one day and then again in one week to push this into your long term memory.

**P**roduct Backlog
**S**print backlog
**I**ncrement

# 60 MINUTE SCRUM

# 4 SCRUM ACTIVITIES

## Sprint

The sprint is a time constrained project phase usually between two and four weeks in length (although sprints of one week are becoming increasingly common). Each sprint provides the opportunity for feedback from the product owner along with other stakeholders which in turn allows the team members the opportunity to adapt or otherwise improve their approach if required.

The sprint is part of the foundations on which Scrum is built, this shorter frequency stage allows for more immediate feedback than traditional project management of software development models allow, providing the ability to change direction in response to changing of emerging user requirements. Sprints of one month or longer are considered riskier than their shorter counterparts due to the increasing risk of changing requirements which is proportional to the duration of the sprint.

There is no prescriptive requirement as to how long a sprint should last although it is generally accepted that they should not last longer than four weeks or less than one week. The sprint length is influenced by a number of factors including:

- The overall project duration

- The amount of risk you are willing to take on (risk appetite)

- The tolerance of the customer

- The ability of the team members

- The experience of the team members (in using Scrum)

The key to each sprint is delivering a potentially shippable product; not a concept, not a working model, but the finished article (or at least one able of being deployed). Essentially this involves being able to close all User stories as complete against the criteria agreed (see Chapter 3: Scrum Aretefacts).

The sprint advances the project incrementally and the frequency of deliverable product shows the value added aspects delivered by the team which promotes the visibility of the team's achievements to date and is appreciated by stakeholders.

Whilst the Scrum framework has been designed to embrace and even thrive in changing environments, it is important to ensure during the sprint that no changes are introduced that would have a material impact on the Scrum goals; this would result in premature sprint cancellation, the scope can however be clarified and renegotiated during a live sprint if the team members reach a consensus.

Each sprint could be considered a project in itself, beginning with a sprint planning meeting and ending with a sprint retrospective and delivering incremental value in between. The sprint allows the team members the opportunity to focus on delivering the backlog items committed to the sprint backlog.

The sprint contains four prescribed activities:

| Sprint | | | |
| --- | --- | --- | --- |
| Sprint Planning Meeting | Daily Scrum | Sprint Review | Sprint Retrospective |

## Sprint planning meeting

The sprint planning meeting is always the immediate first stage of any sprint, which is usually broken down into two distinct parts:

- The team committing to the number of user stories that it will deliver in the upcoming sprint, and;

- Identifying the underlying tasks to deliver this value

The product owner leads the first half of the meeting and will help guide the team members in selecting only the highest priority user stories. The team decides the actual work they will be doing during the sprint. After all, who is better placed to determine the amount of effort required to deliver the Story than the specialist who will be completing the work?

The product owner decides what stories will be considered and typically walks through the user stories and presents them to the team members along with acceptance criteria associated with the Story, at the end of the story it is commonplace for the team to discuss and agree if the Story is in or out of this sprint run; it is essential that the whole team buys into this stage of the project and commits both individually and collectively to delivering the value agreed upon.

This process is repeated until all of the stories have been presented or the team has committed up to its maximum capacity within the sprint timeframe.

In the second half of the meeting the team deconstructs all of the backlog items with a view to break it down into individual tasks (individual in the sense of the task, not the responsibility of the completion of the task). If required the product owner will be on hand to provide any additional information or feedback as required including acceptance criteria i.e. how do we define this task as being complete?

There may be cases where the scope of the user story will be negotiated as a compromise, and the user story may be broken down into two User stories part of which will be completed in subsequent sprints.

It is not unusual for team members to take on more work if they feel they have additional capacity once they have identified the sum of the detailed work required in this sprint– it is also common and permissible for the team to move committed User stories back to the product backlog if they do not feel that they have sufficient resource to complete the work required to a suitable level of quality (which should be deemed to be 'potentially shippable') during the sprint.

The output is a series of sprint goals contained within the sprint backlog which includes stories and associated tasks, which all of the team members have committed to deliver.

## Daily Scrum

The daily Scrum, also referred to as the 'daily stand up' due to the brevity of this meeting (usually lasts no more than 15 minutes), is a daily meeting designed to bring the team together collectively to answer the following three questions exclusively:

- What have I done in the last 24 hours? (Tasks completed)

- What am I planning to do in the next 24 hours? (24 hour plan)

- What obstacles (if any) are slowing me down?

Each team member usually speaks for a maximum of two minutes and each team member answers the above questions in turn. It is important to realise that the first two questions are not to be confused with the typical project status reports found in other frameworks but are in fact a public commitment to their peers to complete a piece of work, and an update on the fulfilment of that commitment, this provides the forum for the team to 'synchronise' at regular intervals to ensure that activities are aligned amongst the team members whilst eliminating the need for other meetings.

The final question is designed to identify any road blocks which the team members may be facing, any problems that arise or obstacles identified are not to be resolved during this meeting but are instead flagged quickly for later review with the Scrum master.

It is common practice to invite a wider audience to observe the daily Scrum (or to hold the Scrum in a public, highly visible place) however only the core Scrum roles are invited to speak during this session. Typically the team members will meet directly after the daily Scrum to re-plan in further detail and discuss any areas of concern raised in the daily Scrum, although pragmatic, this is not prescribed within the Scrum Framework.

## Sprint review

The sprint review meeting is one of two

Scrum meetings that formally close each and every sprint. It is often held publicly and customers or key stakeholders are invited to review the incremental value delivered by the team.

This meeting is designed to increase the visibility of the project delivery as stakeholders get the chance to review the features and benefits delivered in the current sprint as well as providing a forum to receive end user feedback.

The team demonstrates stories which have met the teams definition of done (stories that have been marked as complete must be checked and validated prior to this meeting); if there are incomplete stories in the sprint, this information is provided in this forum and then added back to the product backlog

Stakeholders provide feedback and ideas for future sprints, this feedback is designed to help the team adapt their approach for future sprints. It is important to realise that this is not a decision making forum, and is not part of the product backlog grooming process that will further shape backlog items  and is not the time to make new commitments for the next sprint as this would be addressed at the next sprint planning meeting.

**Sprint retrospective**

The sprint retrospective is the final meeting of sprint, facilitated by the Scrum master, which in practice is usually conducted directly following the sprint review. Contrary to the sprint review, this meeting is usually held in private by the core Scrum team and is intended to help the team continually improve the process. In formal project management methodologies this is the equivalent of a lessons learned log, but instead of creating and updating a document this is a living, breathing practical meeting to discuss practical improvements with a view to implement them immediately

To improve future sprints, the focus shouldn't be on what went wrong or identifying blame, but rather finding positive ways to make the next sprint more effective and successful. There are two questions posed at this meeting:

- What went well during the sprint?

- What could be improved in the next sprint?

The output of this meeting is usually one or two strategic suggestions to carry across into the next sprint.

**Summary:**

A visual summary of a typical two week sprint can be found below.

| Sprint Calendar | | | | |
|---|---|---|---|---|
| Monday | Tuesday | Wednesday | Thursday | Friday |
| 09:00-13:00 Sprint Planning Meeting | 09:00-09:15 Daily Scrum | 09:00-09:15 Daily Scrum | 09:00-09:15 Daily Scrum | 09:00-09:15 Daily Scrum |
| | | 16:00-17:00 Product Backlog grooming | | |
| Monday | Tuesday | Wednesday | Thursday | Friday |
| 09:00-09:15 Daily Scrum | 09:00-09:15 Daily Scrum | 09:00-09:15 Daily Scrum | 09:00-09:15 Daily Scrum | 09:00-09:15 Daily Scrum |
| | | | | 14:30-16:30 Sprint Review |
| | | 16:00-17:00 Product Backlog grooming | | 16:30-17:00 Sprint Retrospective |

**Remember:**

There are five activities to remember, to aid your progress I have come up with a simple sentence which, if remembered, will provide a simple aide memoir in recalling these:

"Some Say Project Management Disciplines Seem to Sacrifice Results – Scrum Resolves this"

The first letter of each work in the sentence is designed to help you recall the activities within the sprint (i.e. "Some Project Management" or SPM is designed to help you recall "Sprint Planning Meeting" and so on)

Write down and repeat the above out load until it is committed to memory; repeat this process in one day and then again in one week to push this into your long term memory.

| Sprint | | | |
|---|---|---|---|
| Sprint Planning Meeting | Daily Scrum | Sprint Review | Sprint Retrospective |

# 5 TRACKING PROGRESS

There is no prescribed approach to the sprint execution despite it forming the bulk of the activities within each sprint; there is however a number of widely accepted tools that support the need to provide transparency to key stakeholders with updated information on progress.

Progress is commonly tracked using two Scrum tools:

- Task Boards

- Burn down Charts

## Task Board

A task board is a simple, yet visually powerful way of tracking and communicating workloads and work completed to date to both team members and key stakeholders, they also reduce the risk of a team member unexpectedly missing an item that the team committed to deliver as it is clearly visible for all.

A task board is usually constructed simply with a white board or sheet of flip chart paper mounted on the wall with the following columns:

- To Do

- Doing

- Done

| To Do | Doing | Done |
|-------|-------|------|
|       |       |      |

Typically tasks are written on the white board (or more commonly, post it notes) and are moved from left to right across the columns as the tasks are progressed. This demonstrates progress over a period of time, provides visual motivation for the team, and is often placed alongside the daily Burn down chart to provide an 'information centre' for the project.

## Daily Burn down chart

A burn down chart is a simple and graphical means of tracking and reporting progress within the sprint which displays the amount of work conducted alongside the amount of effort remaining.

STEWART LANCASTER

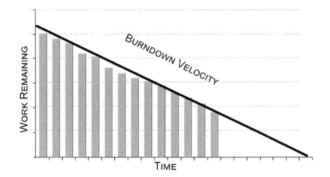

The X (horizontal) axis represents the remaining time within the current sprint and the Y (vertical) axis represents the amount of outstanding work. These charts are often publicly displayed and updated daily as a standard way of communicating progress.

Burn down charts are designed to easily accommodate changes in the workload, allowing the Scrum team to respond positively to change; this is achieved by a sharp (usually vertical) increase or decrease in the outstanding work load:

A decrease in workload is represented like this:

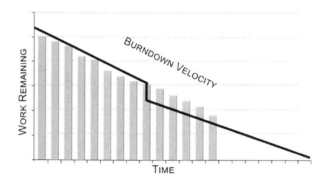

Increase in work load is represented like this:

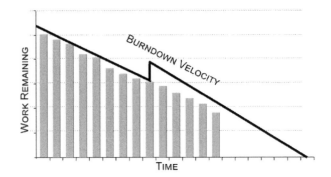

A practical example of how to create a simple burn down chart using Microsoft Excel® can be found in Chapter 8. Scrum Resources.

**Product backlog Grooming**

The product backlog grooming meeting (also known as 'Story Time') is a meeting designed to focus on discussing and improving backlog items in the product backlog for future sprints (backlog items for the current sprint will already be committed to the sprint backlog). It is an opportunity for the Scrum team to define and refine acceptance criteria existing user stories, shaping the overall delivery of the project as well as combining duplicate or overlapping User stories which counteracts the tendency for teams to add as many stories as possible, in a bid for more resource or to make the project look bigger.

It is common for the team to review work estimates for each story as new information is made available on existing backlog items. The output of this meeting is an updated and further refined product backlog.

# 6 ARE WE DONE YET?

One of the most important questions the Scrum team can ask themselves is "How do we know when we are done?", sadly it is a question which is not particularly easy to answer and is dependent on a number of factors:

- Product owner (and customer) expectations

- Clarity of user stories

- Business expectations

- Team expectations

Part of the inherent problem with this question is that it doesn't specify whose perspective of 'done' you are considering; to an Operations Manager the definition of done could be creating a new processes, completing a procedural manual or ensuring all staff have been adequately trained. To a Sales Manager it could mean having a product in the hands of the sales force; to a Marketing Manager it could mean having a product in the hands of the customer. To a Finance Manager it could mean having been paid from the client or perhaps spending the entire allocated budget.

To prevent all of the ambiguity associated with the completion status of backlog items, Scrum teams create the "definition of done" up front so there is no ambiguity as to what is expected and the task can be resourced effectively. It is common for the definition of done to be printed and visualised (often next to task board) which is often in checklist form. It is vitally important to ensure what any definition of done criteria is understood and accepted by all parties.

This common definition provides the team members the confidence to declare a backlog item as complete, where additional requirements are identified (for example at the sprint retrospective) these can be added as new stories to the product backlog.

## Early sprint Termination

There may be times when the sprint needs to be ended prematurely; this could be due to a drastic change in user requirements, a cancellation of a contract or other significant business event. Within the Scrum framework, a sprint can only be terminated early by the product owner. In these instances it is important to still hold a sprint retrospective to gain feedback from this sprint cycle, particularly if the sprint was terminated due to the actions of the Scrum team.

All changes as a result of the work conducted to date during the sprint should be undone i.e. undo software changes to code; revert back to previous document versions. There are a number of instances where early sprint termination is a very positive thing i.e. the customer has identified a new and innovative direction for the product which will provide competitive advantage; this is where Scrum can demonstrate considerable added value, adapting to meet the client's needs in order to deliver the highest value in the shortest available time.

Below is a flowchart that describes the early sprint termination process:

# 60 MINUTE SCRUM

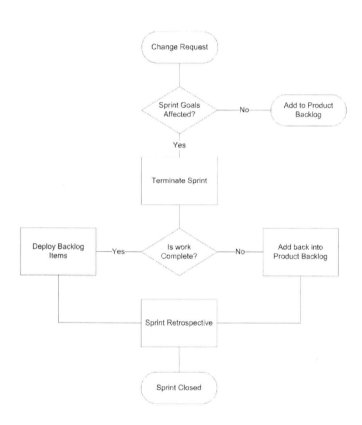

# 7 PUTTING IT ALL TOGETHER

You're now in the final stretch of this book, and by now you will have a solid understanding of the key elements of Scrum. On our journey we have covered the core roles, the key artefacts and prescribed activities that collectively form the Scrum framework.

Below is a summary to refresh what you have learnt and to help put it all together.

## Summary:

Scrum Roles – "PoST"

Scrum Artefacts – "PSI"

Scrum Activities - "Some Say Project Management Disciplines Seem to Sacrifice Results – Scrum Resolves this"

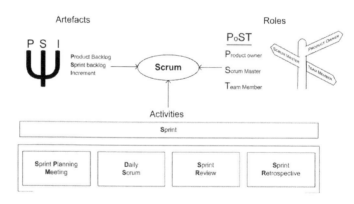

To really increase your chances of successful recall you should draw out the above diagram, adding your own notes, mnemonics or diagrams as you go until you have committed this to memory, repeat this process in one day and then again in one week to push this into your long term memory.

In the next chapter, you will find a number of scrum resources to help you on your journey that you will immediately be able to apply to your activities.

# 8 SCRUM RESOURCES

So you've decided to embrace Scrum with both arms and can't wait to jump into your first Scrum project, below are a list of useful (and in some cases, free resources for help you on your journey).

How long should each meeting last?

There is no right or wrong way when it comes to meeting duration; you want to ensure that all important items are discussed but not at the expense of the end results. The table below provides an at a glance summary to give you guidance on 'ideal' scrum meeting durations.

| Meeting | Recommendation | Example (2 week Sprint) |
|---|---|---|
| Sprint Planning Meeting | 2 hours per week of the Sprint | 4 hours |
| Daily Scrum | 15 minutes per day | 15 minutes per day |
| Product backlog Grooming | 60 Minutes per week of the Sprint | 60 Minutes per week |
| Sprint Planning Meeting | 30-60 minutes per week of the Sprint | 1-2 hours |
| Sprint Planning Meeting | 15 minutes per week of the Sprint | 30 minutes |

Scrum meeting agendas

Below is a list of suggested standard templates that you can adapt and deploy for your own scrum teams.

**Sprint Planning Meeting:**

# 60 MINUTE SCRUM

| | |
|---|---|
| **Meeting:** | Sprint Planning Meeting |
| **Required Attendees:** | Product Owner, Scrum Master, Team Members |
| **Optional Attendees:** | None |
| **Chair:** | Part 1: Product Owner<br>Part 2: Team Member |
| **Duration:** | 2 hours per week of the Sprint |
| **Occurrence:** | At start of Sprint |
| **Inputs:** | Product Backlog, team Velocity |
| **Outputs:** | Sprint Backlog, Sprint Goals |
| **Agenda:** | Part One: High level Sprint planning (i.e. What work will be performed?)<br>• Product Owner discusses the Backlog Items in the Product Backlog<br>• Team Members will ask for further clarity on the scope of Backlog Items from the Product owner<br>• Team Members select Backlog Items for inclusion into impending Sprint<br>• Team Members define Sprint Goals<br><br>Part Two: detailed Sprint Planning (i.e. How will the work be performed?)<br>• Team Members determine how they will deliver the Backlog Items within the Sprint<br>• Team Members agree definition of 'done' with the Product Owner<br>• Estimations of effort for each User Stories is refined as further details becomes available<br>• Backlog Items may be renegotiated in terms of Scope or may even be removed from the Sprint if the Team Members do not feel that they can deliver them in time<br>• Tasks are allocated amongst the Team Members by the team as they begin to self-organise<br>• Product Owner may provide additional information or further clarity regarding Backlog Items if requested |

# Daily Scrum

| Meeting: | Daily Scrum |
|---|---|
| Required Attendees: | Scrum Master, Team Members |
| Optional Attendees: | Product Owner (others may attend but are not invited to speak) |
| Chair: | Scrum Master |
| Duration: | 15 minutes |
| Occurrence: | Daily |
| Inputs: | No artefacts |
| Outputs: | No artefacts |
| Agenda: | 3 questions<br><br>• What did you do yesterday?<br>• What are you planning on doing today?<br>• Is there anything in your way? |

# Product backlog Grooming

| Meeting: | Product backlog Grooming |
|---|---|
| Required Attendees: | Product Owner, Scrum Master, Team Members |
| Optional Attendees: | None |
| Chair: | Product Owner |
| Duration: | 60 Minutes per week of the Sprint |
| Occurrence: | Weekly |
| Inputs: | Product backlog |
| Outputs: | (updated) Product backlog |
| Agenda: | • Write new User Stories<br>• Provide additional detail and / or estimations to existing User Stories<br>• Refine acceptance criteria |

# Sprint review

| Meeting: | Sprint Review |
| --- | --- |
| Required Attendees: | Product Owner, Scrum Master, Team Members |
| Optional Attendees: | (others may attend) |
| Chair: | Product Owner |
| Duration: | 30-60 minutes per week of the Sprint |
| Occurrence: | At end of Sprint |
| Inputs: | Increment |
| Outputs: | Feedback |
| Agenda: | Product Owner:<br><br>• Reviews what has and hasn't met the definition of done during the Sprint.<br>• Discusses the current product backlog<br><br>Team members:<br><br>• Discusses any issues that arose during the Sprint and how they were resolved.<br>• Demonstration of completed work and a Q&A session on the increment |

# Sprint retrospective

| | |
|---|---|
| **Meeting:** | Sprint Retrospective |
| **Required Attendees:** | Scrum Master, Team Members |
| **Optional Attendees:** | Product Owner |
| **Chair:** | Team Members |
| **Duration:** | 15 minutes per week of the Sprint |
| **Occurrence:** | At end of Sprint |
| **Inputs:** | Increment, Feedback from Sprint Review |
| **Outputs:** | Continuous Improvement ideas |
| **Agenda:** | Review last sprint<br><br>• what went well?<br>• What didn't go so well?<br>• How can we improve future sprints? |

Creating a burn down chart in Microsoft Excel®

## Sample Data

# 60 MINUTE SCRUM

| Burned down | | | Balance | |
|---|---|---|---|---|
| Day | Expected | Actual | Expected | Actual |
| 0 | | | 500 | 500 |
| 1 | 25 | 30 | 475 | 470 |
| 2 | 25 | 26 | 450 | 444 |
| 3 | 25 | 24 | 425 | 420 |
| 4 | 25 | 23 | 400 | 397 |
| 5 | 25 | 23 | 375 | 374 |
| 6 | 25 | 21 | 350 | 353 |
| 7 | 25 | 27 | 325 | 326 |
| 8 | 25 | 22 | 300 | 304 |
| 9 | 25 | 22 | 275 | 282 |
| 10 | 25 | 23 | 250 | 259 |
| 11 | 25 | 23 | 225 | 236 |
| 12 | 25 | 24 | 200 | 212 |
| 13 | 25 | 25 | 175 | 187 |
| 14 | 25 | 21 | 150 | 166 |
| 15 | 25 | 21 | 125 | 145 |
| 16 | 25 | 28 | 100 | 117 |
| 17 | 25 | 28 | 75 | 89 |
| 18 | 25 | 31 | 50 | 58 |
| 19 | 25 | 31 | 25 | 27 |
| 20 | 25 | 27 | 0 | 0 |

## Sample Formulae:

| Day | Burned down Expected | Actual | Expected | Balance Actual |
|---|---|---|---|---|
| 0 | | | 500 | 500 |
| 1 | 25 | 30 | =$D$3-SUM($B$4:B4) | =IF(C4="","-",$E$3-SUM($C$4:C4)) |
| 2 | 25 | 26 | =$D$3-SUM($B$4:B5) | =IF(C5="","-",$E$3-SUM($C$4:C5)) |
| 3 | 25 | 24 | =$D$3-SUM($B$4:B6) | =IF(C6="","-",$E$3-SUM($C$4:C6)) |
| 4 | 25 | 23 | =$D$3-SUM($B$4:B7) | =IF(C7="","-",$E$3-SUM($C$4:C7)) |
| 5 | 25 | 23 | =$D$3-SUM($B$4:B8) | =IF(C8="","-",$E$3-SUM($C$4:C8)) |
| 6 | 25 | 21 | =$D$3-SUM($B$4:B9) | =IF(C9="","-",$E$3-SUM($C$4:C9)) |
| 7 | 25 | 27 | =$D$3-SUM($B$4:B10) | =IF(C10="","-",$E$3-SUM($C$4:C10)) |
| 8 | 25 | 22 | =$D$3-SUM($B$4:B11) | =IF(C11="","-",$E$3-SUM($C$4:C11)) |
| 9 | 25 | 22 | =$D$3-SUM($B$4:B12) | =IF(C12="","-",$E$3-SUM($C$4:C12)) |
| 10 | 25 | 23 | =$D$3-SUM($B$4:B13) | =IF(C13="","-",$E$3-SUM($C$4:C13)) |
| 11 | 25 | 23 | =$D$3-SUM($B$4:B14) | =IF(C14="","-",$E$3-SUM($C$4:C14)) |
| 12 | 25 | 24 | =$D$3-SUM($B$4:B15) | =IF(C15="","-",$E$3-SUM($C$4:C15)) |
| 13 | 25 | 25 | =$D$3-SUM($B$4:B16) | =IF(C16="","-",$E$3-SUM($C$4:C16)) |
| 14 | 25 | 21 | =$D$3-SUM($B$4:B17) | =IF(C17="","-",$E$3-SUM($C$4:C17)) |
| 15 | 25 | 21 | =$D$3-SUM($B$4:B18) | =IF(C18="","-",$E$3-SUM($C$4:C18)) |
| 16 | 25 | 28 | =$D$3-SUM($B$4:B19) | =IF(C19="","-",$E$3-SUM($C$4:C19)) |
| 17 | 25 | 28 | =$D$3-SUM($B$4:B20) | =IF(C20="","-",$E$3-SUM($C$4:C20)) |
| 18 | 25 | 31 | =$D$3-SUM($B$4:B21) | =IF(C21="","-",$E$3-SUM($C$4:C21)) |
| 19 | 25 | 31 | =$D$3-SUM($B$4:B22) | =IF(C22="","-",$E$3-SUM($C$4:C22)) |
| 20 | 25 | 27 | =$D$3-SUM($B$4:B23) | =IF(C23="","-",$E$3-SUM($C$4:C23)) |

Example burn down chart based on the above data set:

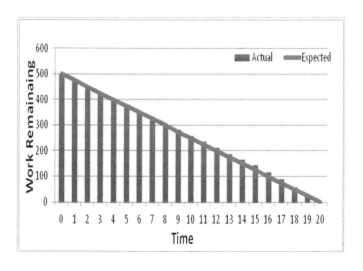

## Scrum Software

## OnTime Scrum

OnTimeScrum from Axosoft allows you to manage Agile based projects, providing help desk functionality and collaboration tools. Paid for services with a free trial. Available at:

http://www.ontimenow.com/scrum

## Scrumwise

Scrumwise provides web based Scrum software including Task Board and Burn down chart functionality allowing you to track resource estimation and progress within the sprint. Paid for services with a free trial. Available at:

http://www.scrumwise.com/

## ScrumDo

ScrumDo is a web based Scrum platform that allows you to create product and sprint backlogs as well as tracking progress through a range of charts. It provides a useful feature that allows you to export into Microsoft Excel®. Paid for services with a free trial. Available at:

http://www.scrumdo.com/

## Scrumninja

ScrumNinja describes itself as the world's most elegant, intuitive, easy-to-use agile tool. Paid for services with a free trial.

STEWART LANCASTER

Available at:

http://www.scrumninja.com/scrum-
software

# 9 GLOSSARY

**Artefacts**

Refers to the one or all of the following: the product backlog, the sprint backlog or the Increment

**Backlog Item**

See User Story

**Burn Down Chart**

A chart that displays the team's progress during the course of a sprint.

**Daily Scrum**

The daily Scrum is one of the five Scrum Activities. This meeting is held between the Scrum team to allow the team to update and 'synchronise' with each other. It lasts no more than 15 minutes.

**Daily Stand Up**

See daily Scrum

**Definition of done**

User acceptance criteria that is agreed upon up front by the scrum team. This is used at the end of the sprint to determine how many user stories can be considered complete

## Early sprint Termination

Sometimes referred to as Abnormal sprint Termination. This is where the product owner ends the current sprint. Common causes for Early sprint Termination include drastic or strategic changes which undermines the value to be delivered in the current sprint. Early sprint Termination should always be followed immediately with a sprint retrospective.

## Increment

The sum of the collective output during any given sprint

## Obstacle

Also referred to as 'road-block' or 'impediment'. This refers to anything that could prevent a team member from delivering any of the backlog items.

**Product owner**

The role responsible for 'what' Scrum team delivers; they own and maintain the product backlog along with the vision of the project.

**Roles**

Refers to any one of the Product owner, Scrum master or the team members within the Scrum Framework. There are no recognised roles outside of these.

**ScrumBut**

ScrumBut is a term used to describe the approach where the Scrum method has been adapted to meet the needs of the organisation.

**Scrum master**

The role responsible for ensuring the team operates efficiently. The Scrum master acts as a servant leader, removing any obstacles in the team's way.

**Scrum team**

The totally of the product owner, Scrum master and team member roles.

**Sprint**

The sprint is a time-boxed period (typically between 2–4 weeks in duration) within the overall project where the backlog items within the sprint backlog will be delivered.

## Sprit planning meeting

The first Activity within any given sprint. The sprint Planning Meeting allows the Scrum team to determine what they will deliver and how it will be achieved.

## Sprint retrospective

The final Scrum Activity, the sprint retrospective allows the Scrum team to review the last sprint and come up with ideas for continuous improvement to be delivered in future sprints.

## Sprint review

One of the two final Scrum Activities

within each sprint which allows key stakeholders to review the Increment delivered in the sprint.

## Team member

An individual who forms part of a multi-functional team, responsible to delivering all backlog items committed to within each sprint.

## Product backlog

The product backlog is the sum of all of the backlog items, change requests, bugs and features related to the project that have not been deliver and are not currently work in progress.

## Sprint backlog

The sprint backlog is a list containing all of the backlog items the team members have committed to deliver in the upcoming sprint.

## Tasks

A task is the smallest unit of work and is usually reference in terms of the number of hour's effort required for completion. It is common practice for User stories to be broken down into tasks by the team members during the sprint Planning Meeting.

## User Story

A statement of requirements in a format that is intuitively understood by stakeholders. Users Stories are first captured on the product backlog before being moved to eh sprint backlog once committed to by the team.

**Velocity**

Velocity is an average measure of how much the Scrum team can complete in any given sprint. It is used to guide the team in the sprint Planning meeting to provide a reference point for the amount of work they can successfully deliver. Velocity is usually measured in Story Points per sprint.

# ABOUT THE AUTHOR

Stewart is an award winning Chartered Manager, qualified Accountant and Project Manager with a number of year's professional experience delivering business change and managing complex projects within the Financial Services industry where he has successful deployed Scrum to manage multi million pound projects for regulated multi-national organisations and listed PLCs.

# ALSO BY THIS AUTHOR

60 Minute: Exam Success

60 Minute Exam Success provides an easy to follow framework that greatly increase your chances of success in your upcoming exam. The book walks you through a number of approaches to amplify our own revision efforts, giving you the best chances of exam success in the minimum amount of time. This book has been engineered to be read in less than an hour, but its benefits will last you a lifetime.

ISBN: 1497516978

Available on: Kindle. iBooks, Audible, Barnes & Noble, Nook and other popular e-readers.

60 Minute: Public Speaking

60 Minute Public Speaking is designed to help you overcome your fear of public speaking in less than 60 minutes. The book is designed to teach you how to create powerful content and to deliver a compelling speech in any situation using the easy to follow, step by step principles.

ISBN: 1499376839

Available on: Kindle. iBooks, Audible, Barnes & Noble, Nook and other popular e-readers.

# 60 MINUTE SCRUM

15969370R00061

Printed in Great Britain
by Amazon